# SUMMER SCHOOL
## in-a-book
### Grades 3-4

written by Marj Milano
illustrated by Priscilla Burris

MARJ MILANO received a Bachelor of Science degree from Boston College and a Master of Arts in Reading Specialization from Suffolk University. She is an experienced teacher in the elementary grades and has done writing and editing in the educational field. She is currently a reading consultant in Watertown, Massachusetts.

PRISCILLA BURRIS received an Associate of Arts degree in Creative Design from the Fashion Institute of Design and Merchandising in Los Angeles. As a free lance artist of child-related artwork, she has been drawing since she was one year old. Priscilla lives in Southern California.

ISBN 0-933606-33-8

# SUMMER SCHOOL IN-A-BOOK
## Grades 3-4

The following series of lessons provide a much-needed motivating way for students to maintain the basic skills they have learned this past year in school.

The lessons are divided into eight units for an eight-week summer skills program. Each unit starts off with an art activity followed by four pages of basic skills practice and review.

To keep up with the theme of each week's unit, it is suggested that children complete each unit in its entirety before going on to the next week's unit.

SUMMER SCHOOL IN-A-BOOK is perfect for long car trips, 'nothing-to-do' afternoons at home, vacation stimulators, and backyard busywork.

A complete answer key will be found in the back of the book. You may want to remove it before your child begins work.

## CONTENTS

Measurements have been converted to metric and are approximate equivalents.

# LET'S GO FOR A BIKE RIDE

Summer is a great time to ride your bike! Of course, the more you ride, the better rider you'll become. Likewise, the more you practice your skills, the better student you'll be. In this first unit, you'll have the chance to . . .

☐ create a city-cycler silhouette
☐ review place value and add
☐ complete a synonym crossword puzzle
☐ write number words
☐ identify kinds of sentences

To get started, let's draw a bike rider on a city street. You'll need a 9''x12'' (23 cm x 30 cm) piece of blue construction paper, a 4½''x6'' (11 cm x 15 cm) piece of black construction paper, a piece of the classified section of a newspaper, some liquid starch, colored chalk, scissors, and a paint brush.

Cut buildings from the piece of newspaper.

Draw and cut the silhouette of a bicycle and rider from the black construction paper.

Place the buildings on the paper, one at a time, and cover each with liquid starch.

Paint one final coat of liquid starch onto the picture.

With the colored chalk, add such details as windows, signs, chimneys, and clouds.

Finally, glue on the silhouette of the bicycle and rider.

The picture is ready to hang.

# PEDAL ON!

Write the numeral.

4 tens and 5 ones
_45_

6 tens and 7 ones
_67_

5 hundreds and 2 tens
_520_

2 thousands, 4 hundreds and 8 tens
_2,480_

8 thousands and 9 ones
_8,009_

3 hundreds, 2 tens and 7 ones
_327_

7 thousands, 4 hundreds, 9 tens and 6 ones
_7,496_

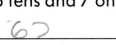

| ADD | | | |
|---|---|---|---|
| 465<br>+723<br>_1,188_ | 1587<br>+6912<br>_8,499_ | 3768<br>+2719<br>_6,487_ | 8616<br>+7538<br>_16,154_ |
| 526<br>958<br>+476<br>_1,960_ | 243<br>417<br>+876<br>_1,536_ | 658<br>759<br>+364<br>_1,781_ | 4882<br>7205<br>+8694<br>_2,5781_ |

Write the next five numbers in each sequence.

2, 4, 6, 8, _10_, _12_, _14_, _16_, _18_

5, 10, 15, 20, _25_, _30_, _35_, _40_, _45_

2, 4, 8, 16, _32_, _64_, _128_, _256_, _512_

11, 21, 31, 41, _51_, _61_, _71_, _81_, _91_

2, 5, 9, 12, 16, _19_, _23_, _26_, _30_, _33_

7, 8, 10, 13, 17, 22, _28_, _35_, _43_, _52_, _63_

4, 12, 20, 28, 36, _44_, _52_, _60_, _68_, _76_

Skill: Reviewing place value, addition, sequencing

# ROAD RACE CROSSWORD PUZZLE

Write the synonym for each word in the puzzle.

## ACROSS

1. find
4. mend
5. uneven
6. lawn
8. exist
9. lift
13. tired
14. race
16. dinner
17. uncooked

## DOWN

1. risk
2. near
3. mistake
4. a fruit
7. clever
10. bring in
11. female sheep
12. journey
13. intelligent
15. metal
18. you and I

Skill: Finding synonyms

# NUMBERS IN YOUR LIFE

Write the words that stand for these numbers.

12  *twelve*                              9  *nine*

18  *eighteen*                           14  _____

20  *tw*                                 41  _____

11  _____                     17  _____

35  _____                     52  _____

Some numbers are used to put things in order. Make these words by adding **-th** to the words below. Write the words. (*The endings of some words must be changed.)

*twenty  _____        *five    _____

six      _____         eleven   _____

thirteen _____         sixteen  _____

*nine    _____         four     _____

seven    _____        *twelve   _____

How would you write these words to show order?

one      _____

two      _____

three    _____

Skill: Writing number words

# LET'S LEARN ABOUT SENTENCES

On the line next to each sentence, write whether it is *declarative*, *interrogative*, *exclamatory* or *imperative*. Put the correct punctuation mark after each sentence. *Remember!*

- A declarative sentence makes a statement and ends with a period.
- An interrogative sentence asks a question and ends with a question mark.
- An exclamatory sentence expresses strong feeling or surprise and ends with an exclamation mark.
- An imperative sentence gives a command and ends with a period.

| | |
|---|---|
| _____ | 1. Let's ride along the bike trail |
| _____ | 2. The path circles the lake |
| _____ | 3. Did you notice the sailboat |
| _____ | 4. What a day for a ride |
| _____ | 5. Turn left at the bridge |
| _____ | 6. What's the problem, Jay |
| _____ | 7. You have a flat tire |
| _____ | 8. Stop here and I'll fix it |
| _____ | 9. Don't you have a pump |
| _____ | 10. Who brought the lunch |
| _____ | 11. This is a delicious sandwich |
| _____ | 12. How long have we been riding |
| _____ | 13. We must be home by five o'clock |
| _____ | 14. It certainly is cool in the shade |
| _____ | 15. Sandy is always lagging behind |
| _____ | 16. Can't you pedal any faster |
| _____ | 17. Watch out for the tree |
| _____ | 18. Are you positive you're alright |

On another piece of paper, write some sentences of your own. Be sure to include the four different kinds of sentences.

Skill: Identifying kinds of sentences

# TAKE ME OUT TO THE BALLGAME

Even though you may not play baseball, chances are that you've seen a baseball game. It's been said that baseball is as American as apple pie. Just as basic are the activities in this unit . . .

☐ make a baseball player sculpture
☐ subtraction and word problems
☐ division of two-syllable words
☐ reading for details
☐ reading a bar graph

Now, here's your opportunity to become a sculptor. You'll need to gather some materials first: some flexible wire, a tool to cut the wire, gauze strips or an old nylon stocking, plaster of Paris, a container for mixing the plaster, water, newspapers, and scissors.

With the wire, shape the figure of a baseball player at bat. For support, nail the wire to a piece of wood.

Mix the plaster of Paris into warm water in a container.

Soak strips of gauze or nylon in the plaster and wrap them around the wire figure. Let the plaster dry.

Insert a small wooden stick for a bat.

You can also make the figure of a pitcher, catcher, or outfielder. Eventually, you could make the whole team!

# BATTER UP!

Subtract.

| | | | |
|---|---|---|---|
| 651<br>−432 | 783<br>− 25 | 584<br>−196 | 477<br>− 89 |
| 8593<br>−3684 | 9510<br>−6327 | 2345<br>− 768 | 5644<br>−3675 |

Solve these problems.

| | |
|---|---|
| 1.  In their careers, Hank Aaron hit 755 home runs and Babe Ruth 714. How many more home runs did Hank Aaron hit? | 1. |
| 2.  Willie Mays hit a total of 660 home runs and Mickey Mantle hit 536. How many more home runs did Willie Mays hit? | 2. |
| 3.  How many home runs in all were hit by Aaron, Ruth, Mays, and Mantle? | 3. |
| 4.  Wrigley Field in Chicago holds 37,272 people. Shea Stadium in New York holds 55,300 people. How many more people can attend a game at Shea Stadium? | 4. |
| 5.  In 1948, Stan Musial was the National League leader in ''Runs Batted In'' with 131 hits. The leader in the American League was Joe DiMaggio with 155 hits. How many more hits did DiMaggio have? | 5. |
| 6.  How many years ago did this take place? | 6. |

Skill: Subtracting with regrouping

# WHERE DO YOU DIVIDE IT?

Look at each example below. Notice the accented syllable in each word.

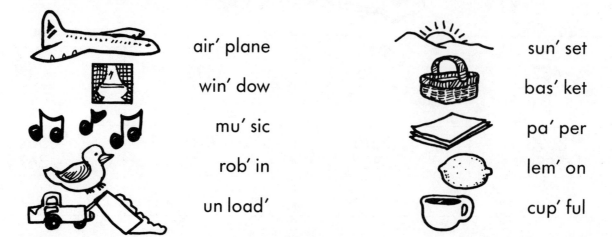

air' plane

win' dow

mu' sic

rob' in

un load'

sun' set

bas' ket

pa' per

lem' on

cup' ful

Divide each of the following words into syllables. Use the above examples to help you mark the accent in each word. The first one has been done for you.

| | | | |
|---|---|---|---|
| baseball | base' ball | fastest | |
| catcher | | seven | |
| outfield | | shortstop | |
| travel | | pennant | |
| careless | | replace | |
| second | | pitcher | |
| notice | | hero | |
| scoreboard | | umpire | |
| middle | | inning | |
| major | | error | |

Skill: Dividing two-syllable words

# A BASEBALL HALL OF FAMER
# HANK AARON

Read the story and then answer the questions.

Hank Aaron was one of the greatest baseball players of all time. Early in the 1974 season, he hit his 715th home run, breaking Babe Ruth's old record. He went on to hit a total of 755 home runs in his career, more than any other player in Major League history.

One of seven children, Hank was born on February 5, 1934, in Down The Bay, a poor section of Mobile, Alabama. He was a quiet, shy boy but he loved baseball. When his family moved to Toulmanville, Hank was able to attend exhibition games by Major League teams at nearby Hartwell Field.

Although there was no baseball team at his high school, he played with a sandlot team on weekends. Once, after a game with the Indianapolis Clowns of the Negro American League, Hank was asked to play shortstop for them for two hundred dollars a month. His mother wanted him to finish high school, however, so Hank waited until he graduated before joining the Clowns. Not long thereafter, he was asked to join the Milwaukee Braves. He wore a Braves uniform for twenty years. During those years, Hank led the National League in home runs four times and won the league batting championship twice. In 1982, Hank Aaron was elected to the National Baseball Hall of Fame.

1. Where was Hank Aaron born? _____

2. Why do you think Hank liked living in Toulmanville? _____
   _____

3. Why didn't he join the Indianapolis Clowns when they first offered him a contract?
   _____

4. How long did he play for the Braves? _____

5. Whose home run record did Hank break? _____

6. Why do you think Hank was elected to the National Baseball Hall of Fame? _____
   _____
   _____

7. Tell who is your favorite baseball player and explain why. _____
   _____
   _____

Skill: Reading for details

# THREE CHEERS FOR THE YANKEES

The following graph shows the number of times each of these American League teams won the pennant during the years 1901–1982.

## AMERICAN LEAGUE PENNANT WINNERS

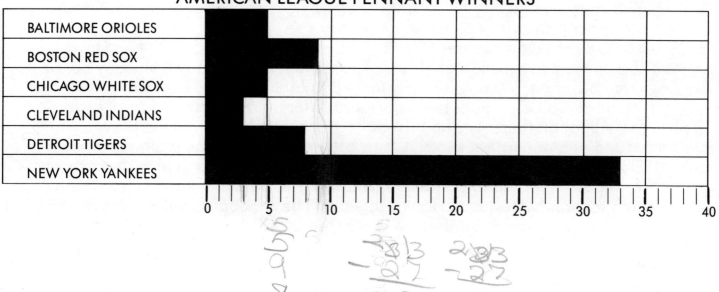

Use the graph to answer the following questions. Circle the correct answer.

1. Which team won the most pennants?
   a. Tigers    b. Yankees    c. Red Sox

2. Which team won the least pennants?
   a. Orioles    b. White Sox    c. Indians

3. How many pennants did the Red Sox win?
   a. 9    b. 5    c. 3

4. How many pennants did the Yankees win?
   a. 9    b. 33    c. 5

5. How many more pennants did the Yankees win than all the other teams combined?
   a. 3    b. 5    c. 7

Skill: Reading a bar graph

# A LEMONADE STAND

A great way to earn a little money this summer is to sell lemonade. Choose a busy street corner, a park, or any place where there are thirsty people and you're on your way to fame and fortune. To help you on your way to success in school, do the activities in this unit . . .

- ☐ make a money box
- ☐ learn multiplication and division facts
- ☐ using capital letters
- ☐ using a dictionary
- ☐ punctuating quotations

You can use a money box to hold all the money you'll make selling lemonade. Here's a simple one to make. You'll need a 9''x12'' (23 cm x 30 cm) piece of oak tag, two 3½''x4½'' (9 cm x 11 cm) pieces, scissors, a ruler, glue, and felt-tipped markers.

Make a box from the large piece of oak tag. Copy this pattern.

Score and fold along the lines, then glue the tabs.

Cut a slit in the top of the box.

Next, draw and color two lemons on the smaller pieces of oak tag. Glue the pieces to the front and back of the box.

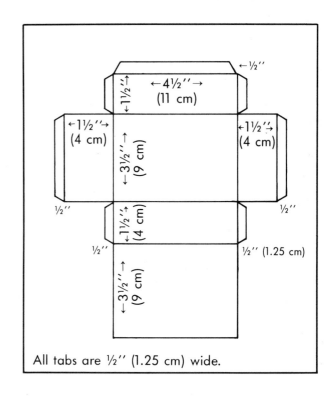

All tabs are ½'' (1.25 cm) wide.

Now, all you have to do is set up a lemonade stand, make the lemonade, buy some paper cups, and you're in business.

# DRINK UP!

**Multiply.**

6 × 3 = _____

4 × 5 = _____

7 × 2 = _____

8 × 9 = _____

5 × 2 = _____

**Divide.**

12 ÷ 4 = _____

25 ÷ 5 = _____

18 ÷ 6 = _____

24 ÷ 3 = _____

21 ÷ 7 = _____

**Multiply.**

9 × 3 = _____

6 × 4 = _____

7 × 5 = _____

8 × 6 = _____

4 × 3 = _____

**Find the missing factors.**

6 × _____ = 18

7 × _____ = 42

8 × _____ = 32

2 × _____ = 16

4 × _____ = 24

**Find the missing factors.**

4 × ___9___ = 36

3 × _____ = 27

5 × _____ = 45

8 × _____ = 64

2 × _____ = 18

**Divide.**

36 ÷ 6 = _____

49 ÷ 7 = _____

27 ÷ 9 = _____

16 ÷ 4 = _____

55 ÷ 5 = _____

**Multiply.**

7 × 9 = _____

5 × 6 = _____

2 × 4 = _____

9 × 9 = _____

8 × 0 = _____

**Divide.**

28 ÷ 7 = _____

56 ÷ 8 = _____

4 ÷ 4 = _____

35 ÷ 5 = _____

63 ÷ 9 = _____

**Find the missing factors.**

_____ ÷ 6 = 9

30 ÷ _____ = 6

_____ ÷ 4 = 4

22 ÷ _____ = 11

_____ ÷ 7 = 7

Skill: Reviewing multiplication and division facts

# FIND THE LEMONS

Write each group of words. Use capital letters where they belong. Some groups of words have no capitals.

1.  april vacation _____
2.  along the mississippi river _____
3.  next summer _____
4.  oranges, lemons, and limes _____
5.  a wednesday morning _____
6.  to seattle, washington _____
7.  on august 16, 1985 _____
8.  president ronald reagan _____
9.  an article about montreal _____
10. a lemon tree _____
11. climbing mount rainier _____
12. italian bread _____
13. the first day of the week _____
14. aunt ellen and uncle malcolm _____
15. phillips elementary school _____
16. along madison avenue _____
17. the barnum and bailey circus _____
18. lemonade and iced tea _____
19. the top of the empire state building _____
20. the lemonade trick by scott corbett _____

Skill: Using capital letters

# A LEMON IS A LEMON IS A LEMON

Write these words in alphabetical order.

orange    apricot

apple    lemon

plum    peach

grapefruit  lime

1. _____   5. _____

2. _____   6. _____

3. _____   7. _____

4. _____   8. _____

These words begin with the same letter. Write them in alphabetical order.

1. _____   5. _____

2. _____   6. _____

3. _____   7. _____

4. _____   8. _____

leader    limit

lantern    locker

lemon    lumber

lonely    ladder

**Guide words** are printed in each lemon in bold type. Circle the four words in each lemon that you would find on a page with those guide words.

**cable**    **cage**
cabbage    comet
cackle    cafe
church    cactus
        cadet

**honor**    **horn**
hood    hope
horizon    hillside
husband    hoof
        heavy

**peach**    **peg**
pencil    pebble
pearl    pedal
peel    peace
        pay

**tide**    **tiny**
tickle    tool
tight    tie
tile    time
        tire

Skill: Using a dictionary (guide words and alphabetical order)

# A LESSON IN COMPETITION

Write the following sentences. Put commas, end marks, and quotation marks where they belong. Remember, a comma is used to separate a speaker's exact words from the rest of the sentence.

1. Let's set up a lemonade stand Jason said

   _____

2. We can earn enough money to buy a new record album Ken answered

   _____

3. But, Toby is already selling lemonade Ken continued

   _____

4. Do you think this neighborhood needs two lemonade stands he asked

   _____

5. Jason answered We'll charge less for our lemonade

   _____

6. Toby just lowered the price of his lemonade Jason observed

   _____

7. Imagine, a price war on Bleecker Street said Ken

   _____

8. Ken asked Shall we lower our price again

   _____

9. No Jason said we won't make a profit

   _____

10. If the three of us join forces Ken offered we can charge as much as we want

   _____

   _____

Skill: Punctuating quotations

# PLANTING A VEGETABLE GARDEN

Imagine having fresh vegetables all summer long right from your backyard! Obviously, you must water, weed, and take care of your garden or the vegetables won't grow. Similarly,, you must tend to your skills or you'll forget what you've learned. Here are some exercises to keep you in practice. . .

☐ decorating garden vegetables
☐ multiplying by one- and two-digit numbers
☐ solving analogies
☐ finding subjects and predicates
☐ using a table of contents

You and your friends can have some fun making a vegetable personality parade. Choose any of these vegetables: cucumber, turnip, celery stalk, carrot, potato, or squash. To decorate the vegetable, you'll need nuts, raisins, carrot and cucumber slices, green pepper, cloves, grapes, lettuce, and plenty of toothpicks. (The toothpicks will be used to attach the features to the vegetable.) Use your imagination to turn a vegetable into a silly creature. Of course, if you're not happy with the results, you can always eat them!

# EASY DOES IT!

Solve each of the multiplication problems. Write your answers in the cross-number puzzle.

**ACROSS**

**1.** 18
× 7

**4.** 618
× 4

**8.** 205
× 3

**DOWN**

**1.** 13
× 13

**2.** 156
× 14

**3.** 13
× 5

| | | | | | | | |
|1|2|3|■|4|5|6|7|
|8| | |■|9| | | |
|10| |■|11| | | |■|
|■|12|13| | |■|14|15|
|16|■| | |■|17|■| |
|18| | |■|19| | | |
|20| | | |■|21| | |

---

**9.** 861
× 6

**10.** 14
× 7

**11.** 23
× 46

**4.** 167
× 15

**5.** 83
× 5

**6.** 854
× 9

**12.** 167
× 25

**14.** 17
× 4

**18.** 281
× 3

**7.** 13
× 2

**11.** 11
× 16

**13.** 273
× 6

**19.** 67
× 38

**20.** 524
× 16

**21.** 269
× 2

**15.** 252
× 34

**16.** 32
× 9

**17.** 15
× 17

Skill: Using one- and two-digit multipliers

# TOMATO IS TO VINE AS CORN IS TO STALK

Choose a word from the word box to complete each analogy. The first one has been done for you.

1. **huge** is to **large** as **small** is to _____
2. **attractive** is to **ugly** as **happy** is to _____
3. **repair** is to **mend** as **part** is to _____
4. **damp** is to **moist** as **ask** is to _____
5. **inch** is to **foot** as **centimeter** is to _____
6. **fact** is to **fiction** as **newspaper** is to _____
7. **add** is to **subtract** as **sum** is to _____
8. **high** is to **low** as **roof** is to _____
9. **inside** is to **inner** as **outside** is to _____
10. **hill** is to **mountain** as **building** is to _____
11. **glass** is to **cup** as **milk** is to _____
12. **kitten** is to **pup** as **cat** is to _____
13. **this** is to **these** as **that** is to _____
14. **window** is to **pane** as **door** is to _____
15. **screwdriver** is to **screw** as **hammer** is to _____
16. **book** is to **library** as **painting** is to _____
17. **elbow** is to **arm** as _____ is to **leg**
18. **baseball** is to **bat** as _____ is to _____
19. **paw** is to **claw** as _____ is to _____
20. **sun** is to **day** as _____ is to _____

| **WORD BOX** | | | | |
| --- | --- | --- | --- | --- |
| club | | | fingernail | museum |
| sad | question | novel | skyscraper | nail |
| dog | cellar | outer | knee | difference |
| piece | coffee | knob | meter | golf |
| night | moon | tiny | hand | those |

Skill: Making analogies

# PARTS OF A SENTENCE

Every sentence has two parts — a subject and a predicate. The **subject** tells who or what the sentence is about. The **predicate** tells what that person or thing did.

Find the right predicate for each subject. Draw a line to connect the two parts of the sentence. The first one has been done for you.

Carol                          was located in her backyard.

The garden                     were still green.

A small fence                  planted a vegetable garden.

Rabbits                        told her to sell some of the vegetables.

Carrots and radishes           surrounded the garden.

Many of the tomatoes           grew under the ground.

Her mother                     had eaten many of the plants.

Write five sentences about gardening. Draw lines to separate the subjects from the predicates.

1. _____

_____

2. _____

_____

3. _____

_____

4. _____

_____

5. _____

_____

Skill: Finding subjects and predicates

# BOOK WISE

The table of contents is at the front of a book. It tells what is in the book. It lists the chapter titles and tells the numbers of the pages on which the chapters begin.

Here is the table of contents from a book, *How Does Your Garden Grow?*

| Chapter | | Page |
|---|---|---|
| 1 | Making a Garden Plan | 11 |
| 2 | Tools and Other Things | 23 |
| 3 | What to Plant | 30 |
| 4 | How to Prepare the Ground | 41 |
| 5 | Planting Seeds | 47 |
| 6 | Helping Your Garden Grow | 59 |
| 7 | Harvest Time | 61 |
| 8 | Getting Ready for Next Year | 72 |

Use the table of contents to answer these questions.

1.  How many chapters are in the book? _____

2.  What is the title of the fifth chapter? _____

3.  Which chapter tells you what tools you will need? _____

4.  On which page does that chapter begin? _____

5.  Which chapter tells you how to care for the garden? _____

6.  On which page does that chapter begin? _____

7.  Which chapter tells you what vegetables to plant? _____

8.  Which chapter tells you what you need to do to the soil before you plant? _____

9.  Which chapter tells you what is the best time to pick the vegetables? _____

Skill: Using a table of contents

# TAKING A CANOE TRIP

Paddling a canoe down a river or across a lake . . . what could be a better way to spend a peaceful summer afternoon! After the trip, find a cool place to sit and do the exercises in this unit. . .

- ☐ construct a canoe
- ☐ finding area and perimeter
- ☐ antonym domino
- ☐ identifying nouns and adjectives
- ☐ writing poetry

If you don't own a canoe, you can make a small model of one. You'll need newspaper, wheat paste, a container, and paint.

Tear the newspaper into small pieces.
Soak the paper in warm water for at least 24 hours.
Drain off the water and squeeze the paper in your hands until you have a pulpy mass.
Mix it with paste until it holds together.
Press the papier-mâché into the shape of a canoe.

Let the canoe dry. Then paint it. You can make a whole fleet of canoes. Paint each boat a different color or paint a design on each one. Small strips of balsa wood make excellent seats.

# HOW BIG?

When you talk about the size of a figure or shape, you need to know about area and perimeter. Area is the number of square units that fit inside a shape. Perimeter is the distance around that shape.

Find the area of each figure below. This ☐ is the unit.

A.

AREA = _____ square units

B.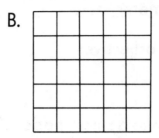

AREA = _____ square units

C.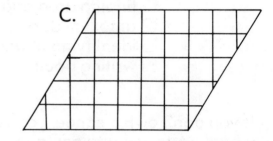

AREA = _____ square units

D.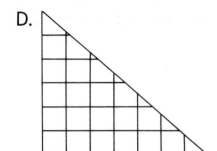

AREA = _____ square units

E.

AREA = _____ square units

F.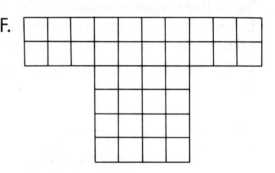

AREA = _____ square units

A simple way to find the area of a figure is to multiply its length times its width.
To find the area of a triangle, multiply length by width and divide by 2.

Use a centimeter ruler to find the area and perimeter of each of the following figures:

A.

A = _____ sq. cm.

P = _____ cm.

B.

A = _____ sq. cm.    P = _____ cm.

C.

A = _____ sq. cm.

P = _____ cm.

D.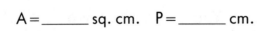

A = _____ sq. cm.    P = _____ cm.

Skill: Finding area and perimeter

# ANTONYM DOMINO

Make a photocopy of this page. Then cut out all 16 squares. Arrange the pieces in a 6''x6'' (15 cm x 15 cm) square so that all the words that touch are opposites of each other.

| receive | simple | friend | |
|---|---|---|---|
| freeze — follow | wide | forbid — succeed | reply |
| expensive | increase | | sweet |
| sour | | fame | permanent |
| open — smile | clean — ask | fail — silent | lead — close |
| | temporary | | fact |
| | decrease | later | cheap |
| cry — dirty | allow | thaw | narrow — foolish |
| donate | | difficult | enemy |
| fiction | | shallow | frown |
| wise — asleep | laugh | noisy | awake |
| wild | sooner | | deep |

Skill: Finding antonyms

# CHARLEY AND THE YELLOW CANOE

An **adjective** is a word that is used to describe a noun. A noun, you should remember, names a person, place, or thing. Write an adjective to describe each noun.

_____ sunset

_____ paddle

_____ day

_____ exercise

_____ boat

_____ flowers

_____ trip

_____ sounds

_____ campfire

_____ summer

_____ apple

_____ leaves

Underline the adjective in each sentence below. Draw an arrow to the noun it describes. The first one has been done for you.

1. Dad bought a yellow canoe.
2. It had seating for three people.
3. He launched it in the early morning.
4. We paddled down the winding river.
5. A green snake slithered on the surface.
6. Birds flew across the rising sun.
7. Tiny ripples lapped at the sides of the canoe.
8. Suddenly, Charley stood up in the narrow boat.
9. The new canoe instantly capsized.
10. We landed in the icy water.
11. I never saw an angrier father!
12. Charley knew he had made a foolish mistake.

Skill: Identifying nouns and adjectives

# POETRY—ORIENTAL STYLE

Haiku (HIGH-koo) poetry is very popular in Japan. A haiku poem has only three lines. The first line has five syllables, the second line has seven syllables, and the third line has five syllables. Here's an example . . .

*A cool summer dawn* (5 syllables)
*Rowing on a quiet stream* (7 syllables)
*I feel the stillness.* (5 syllables)

Now, write some haiku poems. Just remember to count the syllables.

_____ (5)
_____ (7)
_____ (5)

_____ (5)
_____ (7)
_____ (5)

_____ (5)
_____ (7)
_____ (5)

_____ (5)
_____ (7)
_____ (5)

Skill: Writing poetry

# BIRDS AND THEIR HOUSES

Birds are fascinating! You can spend endless hours watching them. To attract different kinds of birds, hang a birdfeeder or a birdhouse outside your window. Later on in this unit, you'll be given directions for making a birdhouse. In the meantime, you'll be. . .

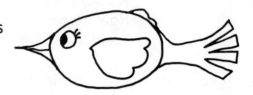

- ☐ making an egg bird!
- ☐ dividing by one- and two-digit divisors
- ☐ identifying verbs and adverbs
- ☐ writing cinquain poems
- ☐ following directions

While you're waiting for the real thing, try making this bird. You'll need an egg, a hat pin, some colored construction paper, glue and waterproof felt markers.

Remove the egg from the refrigerator and let it reach room temperature. With the hat pin, pierce holes at each end of the egg. Enlarge one of the holes by chipping away bits of the shell with the point of the pin. (Make the large hole about 1/4'' (.6 cm) in diameter.) Push the pin inside the egg and stir the yolk well. Put your fingers over the holes and shake the egg. Hold the egg over a bowl and blow through the small hole to force the egg out of the large hole. Rinse the shell with water.

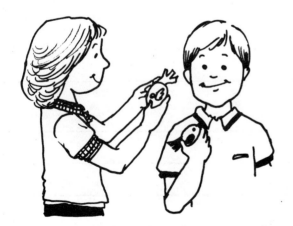

Draw two wings, two eyes, a beak and a tail on pieces of colored construction paper.

Color the egg shell with markers.

Glue the wings, tail, eyes, and beak to the shell.

# BIRD WATCHERS

Divide.

| | | | |
|---|---|---|---|
| 3 ⟌ 42 | 2 ⟌ 448 | 4 ⟌ 496 | 5 ⟌ 855 |
| 8 ⟌ 5304 | 6 ⟌ 4524 | 89 ⟌ 267 | 30 ⟌ 1290 |
| 50 ⟌ 3350 | 26 ⟌ 442 | 34 ⟌ 1904 | 48 ⟌ 3504 |
| 57 ⟌ 2223 | 75 ⟌ 3975 | 82 ⟌ 2214 | 39 ⟌ 1053 |

These birds contain the answers to the problems above. Color a bird when your answer matches its number.

Skill: Dividing by one- and two-digit divisors

# VERBS AND THEIR MODIFIERS

**Adverbs** are words that tell how, when, or where something is done. Write each of the following adverbs under the correct heading.

| never | sometimes | loudly | far | well | outside | then | quietly |
| suddenly | near | now | away | here | gladly | quickly | there |
| downtown | carefully | slowly | late | always | upstairs | today | early |

| HOW | | WHEN | | WHERE | |
|---|---|---|---|---|---|
| | | | | | |
| | | | | | |
| | | | | | |
| | | | | | |

Underline each adverb in the following sentences. Draw an arrow to the verb it modifies. Remember! A verb is a word that shows action. The first one has been done for you.

1. Ella and Elmer worked hard.
2. They hammered the nails noisily.
3. Elmer painted the sides carefully.
4. Soon, the children finished the birdhouse.
5. Elmer hung it outside on a tree branch.
6. Ella placed some seeds inside.
7. Suddenly, a cardinal swooped down.
8. He stayed there for a short time.
9. A bluejay chased him away.
10. The children quietly watched the birds.
11. Later, the cardinal returned.
12. He quickly built a nest.
13. The bird never left his new home.
14. The children gladly continue to feed him.

Skill: Identifying verbs and adverbs.

# POETICALLY YOURS

Let's write cinquain (pronounced SIN-kane) poems. A cinquain poem has five lines and need not rhyme. It tells a little story in a few words. The first line has two syllables and names the subject or title of the poem. The second line has four syllables and describes the title. The third line has six syllables and gives an action. The fourth line has eight syllables and describes a feeling. The last line has two syllables and gives another title for the poem.

Here's an example. . . .

| LINE | SYLLABLES | IDEAS |
|------|-----------|-------|
| 1 | 2 | *Blue Jays* (title) |
| 2 | 4 | *blue, black and white* (description) |
| 3 | 6 | *chattering in the trees* (action) |
| 4 | 8 | *stealing eggs from unguarded nests* (feeling) |
| 5 | 2 | *Robber!* |

Now that you know how a cinquain is done, try some!

_____ (2)

_____ (4)

_____ (6)

_____ (8)

_____ (2)


_____ (2)

_____ (4)

_____ (6)

_____ (8)

_____ (2)

Skill: Writing poetry

# MAKING A BIRDHOUSE

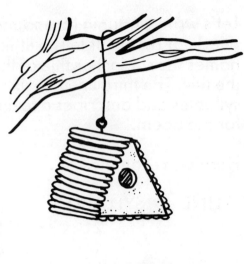

Birdhouses have different styles and sizes for different kinds of birds. Robins, for example, like an open design. Wrens, on the other hand, like a closed birdhouse. To make a birdhouse for a wren, you will need some popsicle sticks, a 9'' (23 cm) square piece of styrofoam, glue, a hook, and some wire. Cut the styrofoam diagonally in half. This will make two triangular-shaped pieces. Cut a hole (1'' [2.5 cm] in diameter) in one of the pieces of styrofoam. Glue popsicle sticks to the bottom of the styrofoam. The distance between the two pieces of styrofoam should be a little less than the length of a popsicle stick. Continue to glue popsicle sticks down each side to make the roof. Put a hook in the top of the birdhouse and thread wire through the hook. You may want to paint the birdhouse. Hang it from the branch of a tree. Don't be disappointed if a wren doesn't make a nest in the birdhouse immediately. Birds will wait to see if the area is safe.

Now that you have read the directions for making a birdhouse, number the steps in the right order.

_____ Cut the styrofoam diagonally in half.

_____ You will need popsicle sticks, styrofoam, glue, a hook, and some wire.

_____ Attach a hook and some wire to the top of the birdhouse.

_____ Cut a hole in one of the pieces of styrofoam.

_____ Then hang it from the branch of a tree.

_____ Glue popsicle sticks to the styrofoam to make the roof and the floor of the birdhouse.

_____ Paint the birdhouse with your favorite color.

Skill: Reading and sequencing

Summer School in-a-book © THE MONKEY SISTERS, INC.

# A TRIP TO AN AMUSEMENT PARK

Don't miss the chance to go to a carnival or an amusement park this summer. You can ride the roller coaster and the ferris wheel, play games, and eat hot dogs and cotton candy. After your trip . . . (if you don't have a stomach ache from eating all that food), do the exercises in this unit. . .

☐ making a jack-in-the-box
☐ solving word problems
☐ writing a friendly letter
☐ identifying word categories
☐ writing a book report

Surprise your family and friends with a jack-in-the-box! To make one, you'll need a 9''x12'' (23 cm x 30 cm) piece of oak tag, a 1''x12'' (2.5 cm x 30 cm) strip of oak tag, a 2''x2'' (5 cm x 5 cm) piece of oak tag, scissors, glue, and paints or felt-tipped markers.

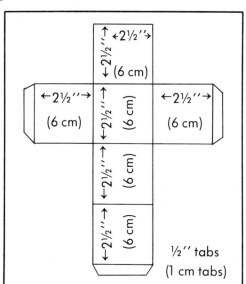

Make a box from the large sheet of oak tag. Copy this pattern.

Score and fold along the lines, then glue the tabs. Leave the top flap open.

Fold the 1''x12'' (2.5 cm x 30 cm) strip of oak tag into accordion folds. Glue one end into the box.

Draw the head of a clown or some other silly creature on the 2''x2'' (5 cm x 5 cm) piece of oak tag. Cut out the head and glue it to the other end of the folded strip.

Close the lid. When you open the lid, the jack-in-the-box will jump out!

# FUN AT AN AMUSEMENT PARK

Solve these problems.

1. Sara, Matt, and Roberto went on the roller coaster. Each ticket cost $1.50. How much did the three tickets cost? How much change would they receive from a five-dollar bill?

| 1. |
| --- |
| a. _____ |
| b. _____ |

2. While they were at the park, the children spent $2.98 for hot dogs, $1.79 for cotton candy, $1.65 for soda, and $.89 for a bag of peanuts. How much did they spend in all? If they had ten dollars to spend on food, how much would they have left?

| 2. |
| --- |
| a. _____ |
| b. _____ |

3. A ride on the ferris wheel is 75 cents. How much more does a ride on the roller coaster cost? If 52 people ride the ferris wheel every hour, how much is spent on tickets in that time?

| 3. |
| --- |
| a. _____ |
| b. _____ |

4. Each hour 325 people enter the park. If the park is open eight hours a day, how many people enter the park in one day? In one week?

| 4. |
| --- |
| a. _____ |
| b. _____ |

5. Roberto paid $2.50 for five chances on a new bicycle. How much does one chance cost?

| 5. |
| --- |
| _____ |

6. Sara's mother bought four pennants for a total of six dollars. How much does one pennant cost?

| 6. |
| --- |
| _____ |

7. Yesterday, 137 children rode on the merry-go-round. Each ticket cost 25 cents. How much was spent on tickets?

| 7. |
| --- |
| _____ |

8. If the total amount of money paid for tickets on the flying saucers one day was $117.30 and each ticket cost 85 cents, how many people rode on the flying saucers that day?

| 8. |
| --- |
| _____ |

Skill: Solving word problems

# WRITE A LITTLE LETTER

Writing letters is the best way to keep in touch with your friends who live at a distance. Rewrite this letter. Place it correctly on the paper. Put punctuation marks and capital letters where they belong. There are four commas and seven end marks missing.

36 sunset lane toronto  canada august 12 1985 dear linda sandy and i rode on the roller coaster today i thought my heart would stop beating sandy screamed during the entire ride i was too busy clutching the bar to yell you should try it sometime it's great fun hope to see you soon your friend ellen

Skill: Writing a friendly letter

# TAKE IT AWAY!

In each group of words, there is one word that does not belong. Find that word and write it on the line.

1.  glass      plate      cup       mug       goblet      _____

2.  tire      brake      chain      roof      seat      _____

3.  bicycle      auto      boat      bus       van       _____

4.  river      road      street      path      avenue      _____

5.  piano      cello      violin      trumpet      viola      _____

6.  orange      bean      tomato      squash      pea       _____

7.  stove      sofa      chair      bench      rocker      _____

8.  ocean      lake      pond      hill      stream      _____

9.  coffee      bread      milk      juice      lemonade      _____

10.  Arctic      Pacific      Atlantic      Indian      Baltic      _____

11.  globe      almanac      dictionary      atlas      encyclopedia      _____

12.  inch      meter      yard      quart      mile      _____

13.  London      France      Spain      Finland      Italy      _____

14.  scissors      pencil      pen       chalk      crayon      _____

15.  heart      lung      arm       stomach      brain      _____

16.  rust      canary      cardinal      robin      wren      _____

17.  huge      enormous      big       large      tiny      _____

18.  Albany      Boston      Nashville      Kansas      Chicago      _____

19.  cardboard      steel      paper      lumber      sawdust      _____

20.  employee      servant      maid      guest      butler      _____

Skill: Categorizing words

# MYSTERY AND THE UNKNOWN

An amusement park would probably make a good setting for a mystery story. Actually, a mystery can take place in any locale. Plan to read some mysteries this summer.

Here are a few for you to solve . . .

*The Green Ginger Jar* by Clara Ingram Hudson
*The Ghost of Follonsbee's Folly* by Florence Hightower
*The Dastardly Murder of Dirty Pete* by Eth Clifford
*Have You Seen Hyacinth Macaw?* by Patricia Reilly Giff

and two stories by Georgess McHargue . . .

*Funny Bananas: The Mystery in the Museum* and *The Talking Table Mystery*

**After reading one of these mysteries**, make a WANTED POSTER based on the criminal in the mystery.

Use a 12''x18'' (30 cm x 46 cm) piece of white construction paper.

Copy this format and fill in the information.

Draw a picture of the character who committed the crime.

Write his or her name. Describe how he or she looked. Tell what crime the person committed, why he or she did it (the motive!), and what clues helped to solve the crime.

## WANTED

RIGHT THUMB PRINT        LEFT THUMB PRINT

Name: _____

Description: _____

_____

Crime: _____

_____

Motive: _____

_____

Clues: _____

_____

Skill: Book reporting

# GLIDING IN A HOT AIR BALLOON

What better way to conclude this book than to take an imaginary trip in a hot air balloon. Just imagine yourself silently gliding over the rooftops and treetops of your neighborhood. Of course, some of you, someday, may actually get the chance to take such a trip. But, all of you can do the exercises in this final unit. . .

☐ create a hot air balloon
☐ write fractions
☐ read a map
☐ graph pairs of numbers
☐ write a story

In the last activity of this unit, your imagination can really take flight. To put you in the mood, make this hot air balloon from paper maché.

You'll need newspaper torn in strips, wheat paste, a balloon, string, paint, six ½"x9" (1 cm x 23 cm) strips of construction paper, and glue.

Pour one cup of wheat paste into ten cups of water. Mix until smooth. Soak the strips of newspaper in the paste.

Blow up a balloon and tie the end securely. Put three layers of pasted newspaper strips around the balloon. When the balloon has dried, paint a colorful design on it.

Next, make a basket from the strips of colored construction paper. Glue three of the strips together crosswise. Glue the ends of a fourth strip together to make a circle.

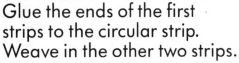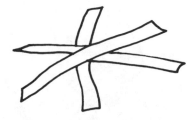

Glue the ends of the first strips to the circular strip. Weave in the other two strips.

Attach the basket to the balloon with string.

# BALLOON BASICS

Color the correct fractional number of hot air balloons. Then write the fraction in numerical form in the box.

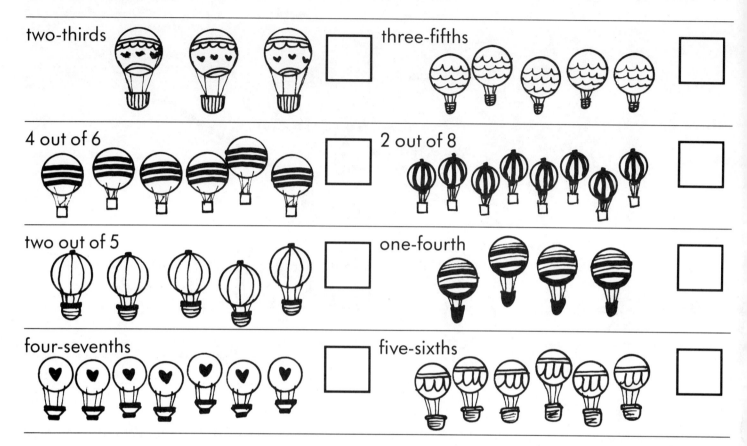

two-thirds          three-fifths

4 out of 6          2 out of 8

two out of 5          one-fourth

four-sevenths          five-sixths

Give at least two fractions to tell what part of each balloon is shaded.

A.

B.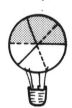

C.

D.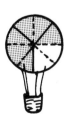

E.

F.

Skill: Identifying and writing fractions

# LET'S GO FOR A BALLOON RIDE

Picture yourself riding in a hot air balloon high above Martha's Vineyard, an island off Cape Cod, Massachusetts. To familiarize yourself with the area, study the map below.

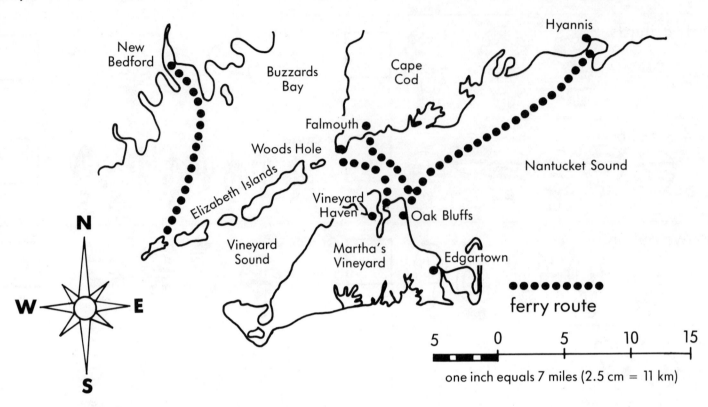

Use the compass rose and the scale of miles to help you fill in the correct answer to each question.

1.  What body of water separates the Elizabeth Islands from Martha's Vineyard?

    _____

2.  What body of water lies to the east of Martha's Vineyard?

    _____

3.  In what direction would you be traveling if you went from Vineyard Haven to

    Falmouth? _____. From Hyannis to Oak Bluffs? _____.

4.  How far is it from Hyannis to Edgartown? _____ mi. or _____ km.

    From Falmouth to Oak Bluffs? _____ mi. or _____ km. From Oak

    Bluffs to Edgartown? _____ mi. or _____ km.

5.  To what two cities can you travel from Oak Bluffs by ferry?

    _____

Skill: Reading a map

# PLOT A SHAPE

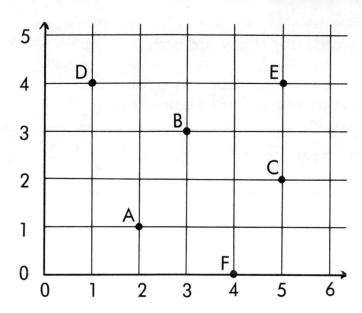

To describe where point A is locted on the graph, we use numbers called coordinates.

The coordinates for A are (2,1).

1.  What are the coordinates for B?

_____

2.  What are the coordinates for C?

_____

3.  What letter has coordinates (5,4)? _____

4.  What letter has coordinates (4,0)? _____

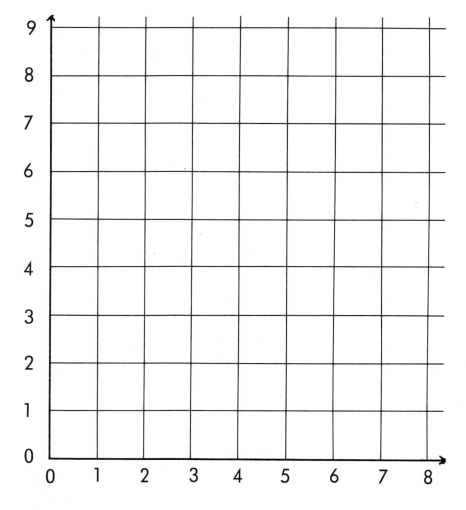

*Make a picture by connecting these points in order.

(3,1) → (5,1) → (5,3) →
(4,3) → (4,2) → (3,2) →
(3,3) → (1,5) → (1,6) →
(3,8) → (5,8) → (7,6) →
(7,5) → (5,3) → (5,2) →
(4,2) → (4,3) → (3,3) → (3,1).

NOW TRY THIS!
Draw a picture on graph paper. List the coordinates for the picture on another sheet of paper. Ask a friend to draw the picture using your coordinates.

Skill: Graphing number pairs

# HIGH FLYING ADVENTURE

Finish this story. Try to include some of the words from the word box.

      The balloon had been attached to the ground by a rope. But suddenly, without warning, the rope parted and we slowly rose into the air. At first, I thought I could _____

_____ but then I realized _____

_____

_____

_____

_____

_____

_____

_____

_____

_____

_____

_____

_____

_____

_____

_____

| soundlessly | landscape | colorful | excited |
| soaring | burst | seagull | coastline |
| frightening | leaking | basket | treetops |
| thunder clouds | helium | wind | drifted |

Skill: Writing a story

# SUPER SUMMER STUDENT

*This certificate is presented to me
for keeping up with my schoolwork
during the summer.*

## Learning has been a ball!

My Name

Grade

# ANSWER KEY

**PAGE 2:**

| | |
|---|---|
| 45 | 2,480 |
| 67 | 8,009 |
| 520 | 327 |
| | 7,496 |

Add:

| | | | |
|---|---|---|---|
| 1,188 | 8,499 | 6,487 | 16,154 |
| 1,960 | 1,536 | 1,781 | 20,781 |

10, 12, 14, 16, 18
25, 30, 35, 40, 45
32, 64, 128, 256, 512
51, 61, 71, 81, 91
19, 23, 26, 30, 33
28, 35, 42, 52, 62
44, 52, 60, 68, 76

**PAGE 3:**

| Across | Down |
|---|---|
| 1. discover | 1. danger |
| 4. fix | 2. close |
| 5. rough | 3. error |
| 6. grass | 4. fig |
| 8. be | 7. able |
| 9. raise | 10. import |
| 13. weary | 11. ewe |
| 14. speed | 12. trip |
| 16. supper | 13. wise |
| 17. raw | 15. ore |
| | 18. we |

**PAGE 4:**

| | |
|---|---|
| twelve | nine |
| eighteen | fourteen |
| twenty | forty-one |
| eleven | seventeen |
| thirty-five | fifty-two |
| | |
| twentieth | fifth |
| sixth | eleventh |
| thirteenth | sixteenth |
| ninth | fourth |
| seventh | twelfth |

first, second, third

**PAGE 5:**

Imperative: #1, 5, 8, 17
Declarative: #2, 13, 15
Interrogative: #3, 6, 9, 10, 12, 16, 18
Exclamatory: #4
Declarative or Exclamatory: #7, 11, 14

**PAGE 7:**

| | | | |
|---|---|---|---|
| 219 | 758 | 388 | 388 |
| 4909 | 3183 | 1577 | 1969 |

| | | | |
|---|---|---|---|
| 1. 41 | 2. 124 | 3. 2,665 | 4. 18,028 |
| 5. 24 | 6. Answers will vary | | |

**PAGE 8:**

| | |
|---|---|
| catch'er | fast'est |
| out'field | sev'en |
| trav'el | short'stop |
| care'less | pen'nant |
| sec'ond | re place' |
| no'tice | pitch'er |
| score'board | he'ro |
| mid'dle | um'pire |
| ma'jor | in'ning |
| | er'ror |

**PAGE 9:**

1. Down the Bay, Mobile, AL
2. He could go to major league ball games at Hartwell Field.
3. His mother wanted him to finish high school first.
4. 20 years
5. Babe Ruth
6. He was an excellent player. He led the National League in home runs 4 times and won the league batting championship twice.
7. Answers will vary.

**PAGE 10:**

1. b. Yankees
2. c. Indians
3. a. 9
4. b. 33
5. a. 3

**PAGE 12:**

| | | |
|---|---|---|
| 18 | 3 | 27 |
| 20 | 5 | 24 |
| 14 | 3 | 35 |
| 72 | 8 | 48 |
| 10 | 3 | 12 |
| | | |
| 3 | 9 | 6 |
| 6 | 9 | 7 |
| 4 | 9 | 3 |
| 8 | 8 | 4 |
| 6 | 9 | 11 |
| | | |
| 63 | 4 | 54 |
| 30 | 7 | 5 |
| 8 | 1 | 16 |
| 81 | 7 | 2 |
| 0 | 7 | 49 |

**PAGE 13:**

1. April vacation
2. along the Mississippi River
3. next summer
4. oranges, lemons and limes
5. a Wednesday morning
6. to Seattle, Washington
7. on August 16, 1985
8. President Ronald Reagan
9. an article about Montreal
10. a lemon tree
11. climbing Mount Rainier
12. Italian bread
13. the first day of the week
14. Aunt Ellen and Uncle Malcolm
15. Phillips Elementary School
16. along Madison Avenue
17. the Barnum & Bailey Circus
18. lemonade and iced tea
19. the top of the Empire State Building
20. The Lemonade Trick by Scott Corbett

**PAGE 14:**

| | |
|---|---|
| 1. apple | 5. lime |
| 2. apricot | 6. orange |
| 3. grapefruit | 7. peach |
| 4. lemon | 8. plum |

| | |
|---|---|
| 1. ladder | 5. limit |
| 2. lantern | 6. locker |
| 3. leader | 7. lonely |
| 4. lemon | 8. lumber |

| | |
|---|---|
| cackle cafe | hood hope |
| cadet cactus | horizon hoof |
| | |
| pebble pearl | tight tie |
| pedal peel | tile time |

**PAGE 15:**
1. "Let's set up a lemonade stand," Jason said.
2. "We can earn enough money to buy a new record album," Ken answered.
3. "But, Toby is already selling lemonade," Ken continued.
4. "Do you think this neighborhood needs two lemonade stands?" he asked.
5. Jason answered, "We'll charge less for our lemonade."
6. "Toby just lowered the price of his lemonade," Jason observed.
7. "Imagine, a price war on Bleecker Street," said Ken.
8. Ken asked, "Shall we lower our price again?"
9. "No," Jason said, "we won't make a profit."
10. "If the three of us join forces," Ken offered, "we can charge as much as we want."

**PAGE 17:**

| Across | | Down | |
|---|---|---|---|
| 1. | 126 | 1. | 169 |
| 4. | 2472 | 2. | 2184 |
| 8. | 615 | 3. | 65 |
| 9. | 5166 | 4. | 2505 |
| 10. | 98 | 5. | 415 |
| 11. | 1058 | 6. | 7686 |
| 12. | 4175 | 7. | 26 |
| 14. | 68 | 11. | 176 |
| 18. | 843 | 13. | 1638 |
| 19. | 2546 | 15. | 8568 |
| 20. | 8384 | 16. | 288 |
| 21. | 538 | 17. | 255 |

**PAGE 18:**
1. tiny
2. sad
3. piece
4. question
5. meter
6. novel
7. difference
8. cellar
9. outer
10. skyscraper
11. coffee
12. dog
13. those
14. knob
15. nail
16. museum
17. knee
18. golf, club
19. hand, fingernail
20. moon, night

**PAGE 19:**
The garden — was located in her backyard
A small fence — surrounded the garden.
Rabbits — had eaten many of the plants.
Carrots and radishes — grew under the ground.
Many of the tomatoes — were still green.
Her mother—told her to sell some of the vegetables.
1-5: Answers will vary.

**PAGE 20:**
1. 8
2. Planting Seeds
3. Chapter 2
4. 23
5. Chapter 6
6. 59
7. Chapter 3
8. Chapter 4
9. Chapter 7

**PAGE 22:**
A. 21 square units; B. 25 square units; C. 35 square units
D. 21 square units; E. 15 square units; F. 36 square units

A. Area = 8 sq. cm.
   Perimeter = 12 cm.
B. Area = 24 sq. cm.
   Perimeter = 20 cm.
C. Area = 22 sq. cm.
   Perimeter = 22 cm.
D. Area = 11 sq. cm.
   Perimeter = 24 cm.

**PAGE 24:**
Answers will vary
1. yellow canoe
2. three people
3. early morning
4. winding river
5. green snake
6. rising sun
7. tiny ripples
8. narrow boat
9. new canoe
10. icy water
11. angrier father
12. foolish mistake

**PAGE 27:**

| | | | |
|---|---|---|---|
| 14 | 224 | 124 | 171 |
| 663 | 754 | 3 | 43 |
| 67 | 17 | 56 | 73 |
| 39 | 53 | 27 | 27 |

**PAGE 28:**

| HOW | WHEN | WHERE |
|---|---|---|
| carefully | never | downtown |
| loudly | early | near |
| slowly | sometimes | far |
| well | now | away |
| gladly | late | here |
| quickly | always | outside |
| quietly | then | upstairs |
| suddenly | today | there |

1. worked hard
2. hammered noisily
3. painted carefully
4. Soon finished
5. hung outside
6. placed inside
7. Suddenly, swooped down
8. stayed there
9. chased away
10. quietly watched
11. Later returned
12. quickly built
13. never left
14. gladly continue

**PAGE 30:**
2. Cut the styrofoam . . .
1. You will need popsicle . . .
5. Attach a hook and some . . .
3. Cut a hole in one of the . . .
7. Then hang it from the . . .
4. Glue popsicle sticks to the . . .
6. Paint the birdhouse with . . .

**PAGE 32:**
1. a. $4.50   b. $.50
2. a. $7.31   b. $2.69
3. a. $.75    b. $39.00
4. a. 2600    b. 18,200
5. $.50
6. $1.50
7. $34.25
8. 138

**PAGE 33:**

36 Sunset Lane
Toronto, Canada
August 12, 1985

Dear Linda,
   Sandy and I rode on the roller coaster today. I thought my heart would stop beating. Sandy screamed during the entire ride. I was too busy clutching the bar to yell. You should try it sometime. It's great fun. Hope to see you soon.

Your friend,
Ellen

**PAGE 34:**
1. plate
2. roof
3. boat
4. river
5. trumpet
6. orange
7. stove
8. hill
9. bread
10. Baltic
11. globe
12. quart
13. London
14. scissors
15. arm
16. rust
17. tiny
18. Kansas
19. steel
20. guest

**PAGE 37:**
two-thirds 2/3
4 out of 6   4/6
2 out of 5   2/5
four-sevenths 4/7
three-fifths 3/5
2 out of 8   2/8
one-fourth   1/4
five-sixths 5/6

A. 1/4, 2/8   B. 1/2, 3/6   C. 9/12, 3/4
D. 6/8, 3/4   E. 1/2, 2/4, 4/8   F. 1/3, 2/6

**PAGE 38:**
1. Vineyard Sound
2. Nantucket Sound
3. north, southwest
4. 28 mi. or 45 Km, 7 mi. or 11.25 Km, 5 mi. or 8 Km.
5. Falmouth and Hyannis

**PAGE 39:**
1. (3,3)
2. (5,2)
3. E
4. F
*Picture is a balloon.